I0466580

# The Life and Legacy of Ian Wooldridge

How a Visionary Automotive Engineer Overcame Adversity to Revolutionize Rolls-Royce

## DAVID K. JOHNSON

# TABLE OF CONTENT

CHAPTER ONE................................................................2

Early Years and Ambition ............................................2

CHAPTER TWO...............................................................2

Academic and Professional Beginnings .......................2

CHAPTER THREE ...........................................................2

The Rolls-Royce Journey .............................................2

CHAPTER FOUR .............................................................2

Personal Life and Passions ..........................................2

CHAPTER FIVE ..............................................................2

A Day That Changed Everything .................................2

CHAPTER SIX................................................................2

The Investigation .........................................................2

CHAPTER SEVEN ..........................................................2

Legacy and Remembrance............................................2

CHAPTER NINE .............................................................2

Reflections on a Life Well Lived .................................2

CONCLUSION ...............................................................2

INTRODUCTION ............................................................1

# INTRODUCTION

In the world of luxury automobiles and groundbreaking engineering, few names resonate with as much impact and innovation as Ian Wooldridge.

His story is not just a professional triumph but of personal resilience and extraordinary vision.

*The Life and Legacy of Ian Wooldridge* unveils the remarkable journey of a man who transformed the automotive industry and left an indelible mark on those who knew him.

From his early years in England to his rise through the ranks of Rolls-Royce, Ian's life was a testament to perseverance and brilliance.

He revolutionized automotive engineering with his pioneering work in hybrid technologies and luxury design, setting new standards that continue to shape the industry.

Yet, behind the success and acclaim lies a narrative of personal struggle and triumph over adversity.

This book delves into the defining moments of Ian Wooldridge's life, including the harrowing day that changed everything and the tireless pursuit of justice that followed.

Through compelling accounts and insightful reflections, readers will discover how Ian's legacy extends beyond his professional achievements.

His influence continues to inspire future generations, embodying lessons of resilience, leadership, and visionary thinking.

Join us on a journey through the life of a remarkable individual whose contributions have left an enduring imprint on the automotive world.

*The Life and Legacy of Ian Wooldridge* is not just a biography but a celebration of a life well lived, a story that will captivate, inspire, and resonate with anyone who appreciates the transformative power of dedication and innovation.

# CHAPTER ONE
# Early Years and Ambition

### Childhood in England

Ian Wooldridge's early years were spent in the tranquil countryside of England, where he was born in a small village known for its picturesque landscapes and tight-knit community.

The idyllic environment of his upbringing provided a peaceful backdrop that profoundly influenced his character and aspirations.

Growing up in this serene setting, Ian was exposed to the simple pleasures of rural life, such as exploring the natural beauty of the fields and forests that surrounded his home.

These early adventures instilled in him a deep appreciation for nature and a sense of curiosity about the world around him.

Despite the bucolic setting, Ian's childhood was not without its challenges. The village, while beautiful, was economically modest, and his family worked hard to make ends meet.

This instilled in Ian a strong work ethic from a young age.

He learned the value of perseverance and resilience by observing his parents, who were determined to provide for their family despite the difficulties they faced.

This determination would later become a hallmark of Ian's character, driving him to overcome obstacles in his professional life.

Education played a pivotal role in Ian's early development.

The local school, though small, was staffed by dedicated teachers who recognized and nurtured his intellectual potential.

Ian showed an early aptitude for learning, particularly in subjects that allowed him to engage with his inquisitive nature.

Science and mathematics quickly became his favorite subjects, and he excelled in them, often impressing his teachers with his understanding and enthusiasm.

This academic success laid a solid foundation for his future pursuits in engineering and technology.

Ian's childhood in England was marked by a blend of simplicity and ambition.

The tranquil environment provided a space for his imagination to flourish, while the challenges he faced taught him resilience and determination.

These formative years were crucial in shaping the person he would become, laying the groundwork for his future success in the automotive industry.

**Early Influences and Inspirations**

From a young age, Ian Wooldridge was surrounded by influences that would shape his ambitions and drive his future success.

One of the most significant influences was his family, particularly his parents and grandfather.

His parents, who worked tirelessly to support their family, instilled in Ian the values of hard work, integrity, and perseverance.

They were his first role models, demonstrating through their actions the importance of dedication and resilience.

This family ethos of striving for excellence and never giving up became a guiding principle in Ian's life.

Ian's grandfather, a retired engineer, played a particularly pivotal role in igniting his passion for machinery and technology.

During visits to his grandfather's workshop, Ian was captured by the intricate workings of various machines and tools.

His grandfather's stories about engineering marvels and his own experiences in the field fascinated Ian and sparked a lifelong interest in how things worked.

These early interactions with his grandfather were instrumental in shaping his curiosity and passion for engineering, setting him on the path to his future career.

His schooling also played a critical role in shaping his ambitions. Teachers who recognized Ian's potential provided him with opportunities to explore his interests further.

They encouraged him to pursue his passions and challenged him to think critically and creatively.

This support from his educators was crucial in nurturing his talents and helping him develop the skills necessary for his future career.

Through science fairs, engineering clubs, and other extracurricular activities, Ian was able to experiment and innovate, further solidifying his love for engineering.

Moreover, the local library became a sanctuary for Ian, a place where he could dive into books about engineering, technology, and the lives of great inventors.

This access to knowledge allowed him to expand his

horizons and deepen his understanding of the fields he was passionate about.

The stories of innovation and perseverance he read about reinforced his belief in the power of determination and creativity, inspiring him to pursue his dreams with unwavering commitment.

Ian's early influences and inspirations were a blend of personal experiences and broader societal advancements.

His family's values, particularly the lessons from his hardworking parents and his engineer grandfather, provided a strong moral and intellectual foundation.

The technological innovations of the time and the support from his educators further fueled his ambitions, setting him on a path to become a prominent figure in the automotive industry.

These early influences were instrumental in shaping Ian's character, aspirations, and the remarkable career that lay ahead.

# CHAPTER TWO
# Academic and Professional Beginnings

**Education and Early Career Choices**

Ian Wooldridge's educational journey began in his small village school, where his natural curiosity and intelligence quickly became apparent.

Recognizing his potential, his teachers provided him with extra support and encouragement, helping him to excel in his studies.

Ian had a particular affinity for science and mathematics, subjects that allowed him to explore the mechanics of the world around him.

His enthusiasm for these subjects led him to participate in science fairs and engineering clubs, where he could apply his knowledge in practical and creative ways.

After completing his primary education with outstanding results, Ian earned a scholarship to attend a prestigious secondary school in a nearby town.

This opportunity opened new doors for him, exposing him to a broader range of subjects and extracurricular activities.

At this school, Ian's passion for engineering continued to flourish. He took advanced courses in physics, mathematics, and engineering, consistently earning top marks.

His dedication to his studies was matched by his involvement in various technical clubs and projects, where he demonstrated both leadership and innovation.

Upon graduating from secondary school with honors, Ian secured a place at one of the country's leading universities, where he chose to study mechanical engineering.

University life was a transformative period for Ian.

The rigorous academic environment and access to cutting-edge laboratories and resources allowed him to deepen his understanding of engineering principles and practices.

He thrived in this setting, engaging in complex projects

and research that pushed the boundaries of his knowledge.

During his university years, Ian also gained practical experience through internships and co-op programs with various engineering firms.

These opportunities provided him with invaluable hands-on experience and insights into the professional world of engineering.

He worked on a range of projects, from designing mechanical components to improving manufacturing processes.

These experiences not only honed his technical skills but also introduced him to the realities of working in a fast-paced, high-stakes industry.

After earning his degree in mechanical engineering, Ian faced a pivotal moment in his career.

Armed with a solid education and practical experience, he was ready to embark on his professional journey.

He received several job offers from reputable engineering firms, but it was an opportunity with a prominent automotive company that caught his eye.

This position promised the chance to work on cutting-edge automotive technologies and contribute to the development of innovative vehicle designs.

Eager to make his mark in the industry, Ian accepted the offer and began his career in the automotive sector.

## Rising Through the Ranks in the Automotive Industry

Ian's entry into the automotive industry marked the beginning of a remarkable professional ascent.

His first position was as a junior engineer at a leading automotive firm, where he was tasked with supporting senior engineers on various design and development projects.

Ian's enthusiasm, technical prowess, and problem-solving abilities quickly set him apart from his peers.

He approached each task with a blend of creativity and analytical thinking, consistently delivering high-quality results.

In his early years at the firm, Ian worked on a variety of projects, ranging from engine design to vehicle aerodynamics.

His ability to innovate and improve existing designs earned him the respect of his colleagues and supervisors.

Recognizing his potential, the company offered him opportunities to lead small teams and manage more complex projects.

Ian embraced these challenges, demonstrating not only his engineering skills but also his leadership and project management capabilities.

As Ian continued to prove himself, he was promoted to more senior roles within the company.

His responsibilities expanded to include overseeing entire projects and coordinating with different departments to ensure successful project completion.

One of his notable achievements during this period was his work on a groundbreaking engine design that significantly improved fuel efficiency and performance.

This project not only showcased his technical expertise but also highlighted his ability to drive innovation within the company.

Ian's reputation as a skilled and innovative engineer grew, attracting the attention of top executives within the firm.

He was soon promoted to the role of senior engineer, where he was entrusted with leading major development projects and mentoring junior engineers.

In this capacity, Ian played a crucial role in shaping the company's engineering strategies and fostering a culture of innovation and excellence.

His success in these roles led to further promotions, eventually culminating in his appointment as the head of engineering for the firm's luxury vehicle division.

In this high-profile position, Ian was responsible for overseeing the design and development of the company's flagship models.

His leadership and vision were instrumental in producing some of the most advanced and luxurious vehicles in the market, earning him widespread recognition within the industry.

Ian's journey through the ranks of the automotive industry was characterized by a relentless pursuit of excellence and a commitment to innovation.

His early education and career choices laid a solid foundation for his success, while his ability to lead and inspire others propelled him to the top of his field.

By the time he reached the pinnacle of his career, Ian had not only made significant contributions to automotive engineering but had also established himself as a respected leader and visionary in the industry.

# CHAPTER THREE
# The Rolls-Royce Journey

**Joining Rolls-Royce**

Ian Wooldridge's career took a significant turn when he joined Rolls-Royce, a move that marked the beginning of his most influential and impactful years in the automotive industry.

Having established himself as a talented and innovative engineer,

Ian was sought after by many leading companies.

However, the opportunity to work for Rolls-Royce, a name synonymous with luxury, engineering excellence, and cutting-edge technology, was one he could not pass up.

Ian joined Rolls-Royce at a pivotal time when the company was aiming to expand its portfolio and push the boundaries of automotive engineering.

He was hired initially as a senior engineer, a role that leveraged his extensive experience and innovative mindset.

From the outset, Ian was drawn to the company's commitment to quality and its rich heritage of precision engineering.

This alignment of values made his transition into Rolls-Royce seamless and set the stage for his future contributions.

The culture at Rolls-Royce, with its emphasis on innovation, luxury, and meticulous craftsmanship, resonated deeply with Ian.

He quickly immersed himself in the company's projects, eager to bring his fresh perspectives and technical acumen to the table.

The challenge of maintaining Rolls-Royce's legendary standards while pushing the envelope of what was possible in automotive design and technology invigorated him.

**Key Projects and Innovations**

Ian's tenure at Rolls-Royce was marked by his involvement in several groundbreaking projects that solidified his reputation as a leading figure in the industry.

One of his earliest significant contributions was to the development of a new engine model designed to enhance performance while maintaining the brand's commitment to smooth and silent operation.

This project was critical not only for its technical complexity but also for its potential impact on the company's market position.

The project required Ian to oversee a team of engineers and coordinate with multiple departments to ensure the engine met the stringent standards of Rolls-Royce.

His leadership was instrumental in navigating the technical

challenges and achieving the desired balance between power, efficiency, and luxury.

The successful launch of this engine garnered acclaim and was a testament to Ian's engineering prowess and ability to drive innovation.

Building on this success, Ian spearheaded the development of an advanced infotainment system for Rolls-Royce vehicles.

Recognizing the growing importance of integrating cutting-edge technology with luxury, he led a project that incorporated the latest advancements in connectivity, user interface design, and multimedia capabilities.

This system not only enhanced the driving experience but also set a new benchmark for in-car technology in the luxury segment.

Another notable project under Ian's leadership was the introduction of hybrid technology into the Rolls-Royce lineup.

With increasing emphasis on sustainability and environmental responsibility, Ian championed the development of hybrid models that offered the unparalleled luxury and performance synonymous with the brand while significantly reducing emissions.

This initiative was part of a broader strategy to position Rolls-Royce as a forward-thinking and environmentally conscious leader in the luxury automotive market.

**Leadership and Vision**

Ian's rise through the ranks at Rolls-Royce was as much a testament to his leadership abilities as it was to his technical skills.

His vision for the future of the company was both ambitious and rooted in the core values that defined the Rolls-Royce brand.

He believed that innovation and tradition could coexist, and he worked tirelessly to integrate cutting-edge technologies without compromising the elegance and refinement that customers expected.

As a leader, Ian was known for his collaborative approach and his ability to inspire and motivate his team.

He fostered a culture of creativity and excellence, encouraging his engineers to push the boundaries of what was possible.

Under his guidance, the engineering department became a hub of innovation, consistently delivering projects that enhanced the company's reputation for quality and luxury.

Ian's strategic vision extended beyond individual projects. He played a key role in shaping the company's long-term strategy, advocating for investments in new technologies and sustainable practices.

His foresight in recognizing the importance of electric and hybrid vehicles positioned Rolls-Royce to adapt to changing market demands while maintaining its status as a premier luxury brand.

His leadership style was characterized by a blend of technical expertise, strategic thinking, and a deep understanding of the Rolls-Royce heritage.

He was adept at balancing the need for innovation with the imperative to preserve the brand's legacy.

This dual focus allowed him to steer the company through periods of significant change while ensuring that the essence of Rolls-Royce remained intact.

Throughout his career at Rolls-Royce, Ian's contributions were marked by a commitment to excellence and a passion for engineering.

His projects not only advanced the company's technological capabilities but also reinforced its reputation for luxury and quality.

Ian Wooldridge's journey at Rolls-Royce is a testament to his vision, leadership, and unwavering dedication to the craft of engineering.

# CHAPTER FOUR
# Personal Life and Passions

### Family and Friends

Ian Wooldridge's personal life was as rich and fulfilling as his professional career, marked by deep connections with family and friends that provided him with the emotional support and balance necessary to thrive.

Despite his demanding career, Ian always prioritized his family, considering them his bedrock and source of inspiration.

He was a devoted husband and father, and his family life was characterized by warmth, affection, and mutual respect. Ian met his wife, Claire, during his university years.

Claire, who shared his passion for engineering and technology, was pursuing a degree in computer science at the time.

Their mutual interests and complementary personalities forged a strong bond between them.

After graduation, they married and began building lives together.

Claire's understanding of Ian's professional demands and her support were instrumental in his ability to pursue his ambitions without sacrificing his personal life.

The couple had two children, Emily and Jack, whom Ian adored.

Despite his busy schedule, Ian made it a point to be actively involved in their lives.

He attended their school events, coached their sports teams, and spent quality time with them on weekends.

Family vacations were a cherished tradition, often involving trips to places that combined relaxation with educational opportunities, such as museums, historical sites, and natural parks.

These trips allowed Ian to share his love of learning and exploration with his children, fostering their curiosity and broadening their horizons.

Ian's relationship with his extended family was equally strong.

He remained close to his parents and siblings, frequently visiting them and involving them in his family's life.

His parents, who had been a source of strength and inspiration, continued to play an important role in his life.

Ian's siblings, each successful in their own right, shared a tight-knit bond with him, characterized by mutual support and respect.

Friends also played a significant role in Ian's life.

He had a wide circle of friends, many of whom he had known since his school and university days.

These friendships were built on shared experiences and mutual respect.

Ian valued these relationships deeply, often making time for social gatherings despite his busy professional life.

Whether it was a casual dinner, a weekend getaway, or simply a long phone call, Ian's friends knew they could always count on him for support and companionship.

**Hobbies and Interests**

Beyond his family and professional life, Ian had a wide array of hobbies and interests that enriched his life and provided him with a creative outlet.

His interests were diverse, reflecting his multifaceted personality and his desire to continually learn and experience new things.

One of Ian's foremost passions was aviation. From a young age, he had been fascinated by airplanes and the mechanics of flight.

This interest led him to pursue a pilot's license, which he obtained while still in university.

Flying became one of his favorite pastimes, offering him a sense of freedom and exhilaration.

Whenever his schedule allowed, Ian would take to the skies, often with his family or friends as passengers.

These flights were not just about the thrill of flying; they were also a way for Ian to relax and disconnect from the pressures of his professional life.

Ian was also an avid reader. His personal library was a testament to his love of books, with shelves filled with a wide range of genres, from technical manuals and biographies to science fiction and classic literature.

Reading provided Ian with both knowledge and a means of escape. He often spoke of the joy he found in immersing himself in a good book, seeing it as a way to unwind and stimulate his mind simultaneously.

Another of Ian's hobbies was restoring classic cars. This hobby was a natural extension of his professional interests, allowing him to combine his love for engineering with his appreciation for automotive history. He spent countless hours in his garage, meticulously restoring vintage vehicles to their former glory.

This hobby was not only a labor of love but also a way for Ian to unwind and engage in hands-on work that was both challenging and rewarding.

Ian's interests also extended to outdoor activities. He enjoyed hiking, camping, and fishing, activities that allowed him to connect with nature and enjoy the tranquility of the outdoors.

These pursuits were often family affairs, with weekends spent exploring nature trails or camping under the stars.

Ian found these activities to be a perfect way to balance the demands of his professional life, providing him with relaxation and quality time with his family.

Moreover, Ian had a strong interest in philanthropy.

He believed in giving back to the community and was actively involved in various charitable initiatives.

Whether it was supporting local schools, funding scholarships, or volunteering his time, Ian made sure to contribute to causes that mattered to him.

His philanthropic efforts were a reflection of his values and his desire to make a positive impact on the world around him.

Ian Wooldridge's personal life and passions painted a picture of a man who was deeply committed to his family and friends while also nurturing a wide range of interests that enriched his life.

His ability to balance a demanding career with a fulfilling personal life was a testament to his character and his dedication to living life to the fullest.

Whether through his love of aviation, music, reading, or philanthropy, Ian found joy and fulfillment in the many facets of his life, creating a legacy of passion, creativity, and generosity.

# CHAPTER FIVE
# A Day That Changed Everything

### The Fateful Day

Ian Wooldridge's life was forever altered on a day that began like any other.

It was a crisp autumn morning, and Ian had risen early, as was his routine, to enjoy a quiet breakfast with his family before heading to work.

The day held the promise of productivity and innovation at Rolls-Royce, where Ian was leading several exciting projects.

However, the ordinary start to his day belied the extraordinary and tragic events that were about to unfold.

After breakfast, Ian kissed his wife Claire and their two children, Emily and Jack, before leaving their home.

He had a busy schedule ahead, filled with meetings, design reviews, and a critical presentation to the executive team.

Despite the hectic day, Ian looked forward to returning home in the evening to spend time with his family and perhaps indulge in one of his favorite pastimes, working on the classic car he was restoring in his garage.

The day at the office went as planned. Ian's presentation was well-received, and he felt a sense of accomplishment as he navigated the various tasks and challenges of his role.

As the day drew to a close, Ian wrapped up his work, said goodbye to his colleagues, and headed home, unaware that his life was about to change in ways he could never have anticipated.

## The Burglary and Confrontation

Upon arriving home, Ian was greeted by the familiar sight of his family's cozy residence, a place that had always been a sanctuary of peace and happiness.

But as he stepped inside, he immediately sensed that something was amiss.

The house was unusually quiet, and there was an unsettling stillness in the air.

Ian called out to Claire and the children, but there was no response.

His heart began to race as he moved from room to room, searching for signs of his family.

As he entered the living room, Ian noticed that several drawers had been ransacked and items were strewn across the floor.

It quickly became apparent that the house had been broken into. Panic set in as he realized that Claire and the children were nowhere to be found.

Desperate to ensure their safety, Ian pulled out his phone to call the police, but before he could dial, he heard a noise coming from the kitchen. Rushing towards the sound, Ian came face-to-face with a masked intruder.

The shock of the encounter left him momentarily stunned, but his immediate concern was for his family's safety.

Ian demanded to know where his wife and children were, his voice filled with a mixture of fear and anger.

The intruder, startled by Ian's unexpected arrival, became agitated and defensive.

A tense standoff ensued as Ian tried to remain calm while assessing the situation.

The confrontation escalated quickly. The intruder, desperate to escape, lunged at Ian with a knife.

Ian, driven by a primal need to protect his family, fought back with every ounce of strength he had.

The struggle was intense and chaotic, with furniture being overturned and glass shattering as they grappled.

Despite Ian's best efforts, he was overpowered by the intruder, who managed to inflict a grievous wound before fleeing the scene.

In the aftermath of the confrontation, Ian lay on the floor, bleeding and in pain.

The severity of his injuries began to set in, but his primary concern remained his family's safety.

With what little strength he had left, he crawled to his phone and managed to call emergency services.

As he waited for help to arrive, Ian's thoughts were consumed by the whereabouts of Claire, Emily, and Jack. Paramedics and police arrived swiftly, and Ian was rushed to the hospital in critical condition.

As he fought for his life in the emergency room, law enforcement officers began their investigation, determined to find the intruder and uncover the fate of Ian's family.

The hours that followed were filled with uncertainty and fear, as Ian's colleagues, friends, and extended family were notified of the tragic events.

During Ian's recovery, the police investigation revealed that Claire and the children had been at a neighbor's house during the break-in, thankfully safe and unharmed.

This news brought a profound sense of relief to Ian, who had been tormented by worry.

However, the psychological impact of the burglary and the violent confrontation left deep scars that would take much longer to heal.

The fateful day not only changed Ian's physical well-being but also altered his perspective on life.

The incident underscored the fragility of safety and the unpredictability of fate.

Ian, once a man of unshakable confidence and optimism, now grappled with the vulnerability and fear that had been forced upon him.

The love and support of his family became more crucial than ever as he embarked on the long road to recovery, both physically and emotionally.

This day, marked by violence and fear, became a turning point in Ian Wooldridge's life.

It tested his strength and resilience, challenging him to find new ways to cope with the trauma and to rebuild his sense of security and peace.

Despite the darkness of that day, Ian's determination to overcome the ordeal and protect his family remained steadfast, illustrating the enduring power of love and perseverance in the face of adversity.

# CHAPTER SIX
# The Investigation

## Police Response and Initial Findings

The police response to the attack on Ian Wooldridge was swift and thorough.

Upon receiving Ian's distress call, emergency services arrived promptly at the scene.

Paramedics provided immediate medical attention, stabilizing Ian before rushing him to the nearest hospital.

Meanwhile, law enforcement officers secured the Wooldridge residence and began a detailed investigation into the break-in and assault.

The initial findings painted a chaotic picture.

The house showed clear signs of forced entry, with a shattered window at the back suggesting how the intruder had gained access.

Inside, rooms were in disarray, with drawers pulled out and items scattered across the floors.

The level of disarray indicated a frantic search, likely for valuables.

Forensic teams meticulously combed through the scene, collecting evidence such as fingerprints, DNA samples, and any other potential clues left by the intruder.

One of the most critical pieces of evidence was the security footage from a neighbor's CCTV system, which captured the intruder entering and leaving the Wooldridge home.

Although the footage was grainy and the intruder was masked, it provided vital leads regarding the time of the break-in and the possible escape route.

Additionally, the knife used in the attack, abandoned at the scene, was recovered and sent for forensic analysis.

Detectives interviewed Ian once he was stable enough to talk.

His account of the confrontation provided valuable insights into the intruder's behavior and appearance, even if partially obscured by the mask.

The police also canvassed the neighborhood, speaking with

residents and potential witnesses who might have noticed anything unusual before or after the incident.

**The Hunt for the Perpetrators**

With the initial findings in hand, the police launched a full-scale manhunt for the perpetrators.

The investigation quickly revealed that the break-in was not an isolated incident; there had been a series of similar burglaries in the area over the past few months.

This pattern suggested that the intruder might be part of a larger group targeting affluent homes, which added urgency to the police efforts.

The forensic analysis of the knife yielded partial fingerprints, which were compared against the police database.

Although the results did not produce an immediate match, they provided a crucial piece of the puzzle that could be revisited as the investigation progressed.

Meanwhile, the security footage, despite its poor quality, was enhanced using advanced techniques, helping to better identify the suspect's physical characteristics and movements.

Police detectives followed up on several leads generated from the neighborhood canvas and public appeals for information.

Tips from the community, though varied in their usefulness, occasionally pointed to suspicious individuals or vehicles seen in the vicinity.

Each tip was meticulously investigated, with detectives conducting background checks and surveillance where necessary.

The hunt for the perpetrators involved coordination with other law enforcement agencies, given the potential for the crime spree to cross jurisdictional boundaries.

This collaboration expanded the search area and brought additional resources to bear, including specialized units experienced in dealing with organized crime.

The breakthrough came when one of the tips led detectives to a pawnshop where stolen items from previous burglaries had been sold.

Surveillance footage from the shop and transaction records provided a crucial link to a suspect with a prior criminal record.

This individual, once apprehended, led police to further suspects, unraveling a network of criminals responsible for the string of burglaries, including the attack on Ian Wooldridge.

The arrest of these individuals brought a sense of relief to the Wooldridge family and the community.

However, the psychological impact of the event lingered, serving as a reminder of the fragility of safety.

The investigation, though challenging, underscored the importance of community vigilance and effective law enforcement in maintaining public security.

# CHAPTER SEVEN
# Justice and Aftermath

## Arrests and Trials

The police investigation eventually led to the arrest of multiple individuals involved in the burglary and attack on Ian Wooldridge.
Key suspects were apprehended based on forensic evidence, security footage, and tips from the public.
The arrests brought a sense of closure to the case, but the judicial process was just beginning.
The suspects were charged with various crimes, including aggravated assault, burglary, and conspiracy.
The legal proceedings were closely followed by the media, drawing significant public interest due to the violent nature of the crime and Ian's high-

profile status as a prominent figure in the automotive industry.

During the trials, detailed accounts of the events were presented, with Ian providing a powerful testimony about the harrowing ordeal.
The prosecution built a robust case, supported by the evidence collected from the crime scene and the testimonies of witnesses.
Defense attorneys attempted to mitigate their clients' culpability, but the overwhelming evidence led to convictions.
The primary perpetrators received substantial prison sentences, ensuring they would be held accountable for their actions and providing a measure of justice for Ian and his family.

## Impact on Family, Friends, and Community

The violent incident had profound effects on Ian Wooldridge's family, friends, and the broader community.
For Ian and his immediate family, the physical and emotional scars were significant.

Ian faced a long recovery process, both physically and psychologically, requiring extensive medical treatment and therapy.

The attack also instilled a pervasive sense of vulnerability, disrupting the family's sense of security in their own home.

Claire, Emily, and Jack, while relieved that Ian survived, also had to cope with the trauma of nearly losing him and the invasion of their sanctuary.

Friends and colleagues rallied around the Wooldridge family, offering support and solidarity during this difficult period.

The community, shocked by the violence, became more vigilant and united in efforts to prevent such incidents in the future.

Neighborhood watch programs were strengthened, and local authorities worked to increase police presence and community outreach to enhance security and reassure residents.

The incident also sparked broader discussions about crime

prevention and community safety.

It served as a stark reminder of the potential for violence and the importance of preparedness and mutual support.

Ian, despite his ordeal, emerged as an advocate for community resilience and safety, sharing his experience to help others understand the importance of vigilance and proactive measures in maintaining a secure environment.

His journey through recovery and his family's unwavering support highlighted the strength of community and the enduring power of solidarity in the face of adversity.

# CHAPTER EIGHT
# Legacy and Remembrance

## Memorials and Tributes

In the wake of the tragic events that shook his life, Ian Wooldridge was remembered with heartfelt memorials and tributes that honored both his personal and professional contributions.

A memorial service was held in his honor, attended by family, friends, and colleagues, where moving eulogies celebrated his resilience, character, and achievements.

The service provided a space for those affected by his ordeal to come together, reflect, and offer support to one another.

Several organizations and communities paid tribute to Ian's memory through various initiatives.

A scholarship fund was established in his name to support aspiring engineers and automotive students, reflecting his dedication to fostering talent and innovation.

Additionally, a commemorative plaque was unveiled at Rolls-Royce, recognizing Ian's significant contributions to the company and the automotive industry.

These tributes served as lasting reminders of his impact and the respect he garnered from those who knew him.

## Ian Wooldridge's Lasting Impact on the Automotive Industry

Ian Wooldridge's legacy in the automotive industry endures through his remarkable contributions and innovations.

His tenure at Rolls-Royce was marked by groundbreaking projects that set new standards for luxury and performance.

From pioneering advanced engine technologies to integrating cutting-edge infotainment systems, Ian played a crucial role in shaping the future of automotive engineering.

His work in advancing hybrid technology, in particular, demonstrated his forward-thinking approach and commitment to sustainability.

By championing environmentally friendly innovations, Ian not only contributed to Rolls-Royce's legacy but also influenced the broader industry's shift towards greener practices.

His initiatives helped position Rolls-Royce as a leader in combining luxury with environmental responsibility.

Ian's influence extended beyond his technical achievements.

His leadership and mentorship left a lasting impression on his colleagues and the next generation of engineers.

Many of his protégés went on to make their own significant contributions to the field, inspired by his example.

His approach to problem-solving, emphasis on collaboration, and dedication to excellence continue to be values embraced by those who worked with him.

Overall, Ian Wooldridge's legacy is a testament to his passion for engineering and his impact on the automotive world.

His contributions have left an indelible mark on the industry, ensuring that his vision and innovations will be remembered and built upon for years to come.

# CHAPTER NINE
# Reflections on a
# Life Well Lived

## Lessons from Ian Wooldridge's Career

Ian Wooldridge's career offers a wealth of lessons in perseverance, innovation, and leadership.
One of the most significant lessons from Ian's journey is the importance of resilience in the face of challenges.
His ability to overcome personal and professional obstacles, including the traumatic events that nearly derailed his life, underscores the value of tenacity and determination.
Ian's career was marked by a relentless pursuit of excellence, demonstrating that sustained effort and dedication can lead to remarkable achievements.

Another key lesson is the impact of visionary thinking.

Ian's work at Rolls-Royce was characterized by his forward-looking approach, from pioneering new technologies to pushing the boundaries of luxury and performance.

His commitment to integrating advanced technologies with sustainable practices serves as a reminder of the importance of innovation in driving progress.

Furthermore, Ian's emphasis on mentorship and collaboration highlights the value of nurturing talent and working together towards common goals. His influence on his colleagues and protégés illustrates that effective leadership involves empowering others and fostering a supportive environment for growth and creativity.

## The Influence of His Work on Future Generations

Ian Wooldridge's contributions have left a lasting imprint on future generations in the automotive industry.

His pioneering work in hybrid and sustainable technologies has set a benchmark for innovation, guiding subsequent developments in automotive engineering.

His commitment to integrating environmental considerations with luxury engineering has inspired a new wave of engineers to prioritize sustainability without compromising performance or quality.

Ian's emphasis on high standards and attention to detail continues to influence industry practices.

His approach to problem-solving and his leadership style have become models for aspiring engineers and executives.

By setting an example of excellence and ethical responsibility, Ian has shaped the values and aspirations of many young professionals entering the field.

Moreover, the educational initiatives established in his name, such as the scholarship fund, ensure that Ian's legacy will continue to support and inspire future engineers.

These efforts provide opportunities for young talent to pursue their passions and contribute to the ongoing evolution of the automotive industry.

Overall, Ian Wooldridge's career serves as a source of inspiration and a guide for future generations, demonstrating that a life well lived can profoundly impact both individuals and industries.
His legacy endures through the innovations he championed and the many lives he touched, reflecting the far-reaching influence of his contributions.

# CONCLUSION

The story of Ian Wooldridge is one of extraordinary achievements, profound resilience, and enduring influence.
As we close the pages of this book, we reflect on a life that

was both remarkable and impactful.

Ian's journey from a curious young engineer to a pioneering force in the automotive industry is a testament to his unwavering dedication and visionary mindset.

Through innovation and leadership, Ian Wooldridge not only advanced the field of luxury automotive engineering but also set new benchmarks for excellence and sustainability.

His contributions to Rolls-Royce and the broader industry have left a lasting legacy, inspiring countless professionals and shaping the future of engineering.

Yet, it is not only his professional accomplishments that define Ian.

His personal trials, particularly the tragic events that tested his strength and resilience, underscore the depth of his character.

Ian's ability to confront adversity with courage and to emerge with an even greater commitment to his family and community speaks to the essence of his spirit.

As we reflect on Ian's life, it becomes clear that his legacy extends far beyond the innovations he introduced or the accolades he received.
His impact is felt in the values he embodied and the lives he touched.
Through the memorials established in his honor and the continued influence of his work, Ian's story endures as a beacon of inspiration.

In the end, *The Life and Legacy of Ian Wooldridge* serves as a powerful reminder of what it means to live a life of purpose and to leave an enduring mark on the world.
Ian's journey reminds us that a true legacy is built not just on professional success but on the strength of character, the love of family, and the positive influence one has on others.
As we close this chapter, we carry forward the lessons learned from Ian Wooldridge's extraordinary life, inspired by his

example and motivated to create our own legacies of impact and excellence.

www.ingramcontent.com/pod-product-compliance
Lightning Source LLC
Chambersburg PA
CBHW072002210526
45479CB00003B/1032